If I Were a Cheetah

By Meg Gaertner

level
2
little blue
readers

www.littlebluehousebooks.com

Little Blue House is distributed by North Star Editions:
sales@northstareditions.com | 888-417-0195

Produced for Little Blue House by Red Line Editorial.

Photographs ©: iStockphoto, cover, 4, 6–7, 9, 11 (bottom), 12–13, 14, 17, 18–19, 20 (top), 20 (bottom), 23, 24 (top left), 24 (top right), 24 (bottom left), 24 (bottom right); Denis-Huot/NaturePL/Science Source, 11 (top)

Library of Congress Control Number: 2020913847

ISBN
978-1-64619-302-8 (hardcover)
978-1-64619-320-2 (paperback)
978-1-64619-356-1 (ebook pdf)
978-1-64619-338-7 (hosted ebook)

Printed in the United States of America
Mankato, MN
012021

About the Author

Meg Gaertner enjoys reading, writing, dancing, and being outside. She loves all wild cats, including cheetahs. She lives in Minnesota.

Table of Contents

grassland

Going for Speed

If I were a cheetah, I would live in dry grasslands.

I would be the fastest land animal on Earth.

I would have short fur with black spots. These spots would help me hide in tall grass.

I would have long, thin legs and a long tail. My tail would help me move in the direction I wanted to go.

tail

leg

I would have hard pads on my feet.
They would help me run quickly.

pads

I would have black markings on my face. They would keep the sun out of my eyes. They would help me see better while hunting.

Hunting

If I were a cheetah, I would hunt during the day.

I would stand on a rock and look for food.

I would go from standing still to racing in just three seconds.
I would turn quickly while chasing my food.

I would be very tired after the chase, and I would need to rest.

Then I would eat quickly before other animals could steal my food.

Other Behaviors

If I were a cheetah, I would eat antelopes.

But I would also eat smaller animals such as hares and birds.

I would have three to five cubs.

I would leave them alone to find food for them.

Once they were older, I would teach them how to hunt like I do.

Glossary

antelope

grassland

cubs

tail

Index